TOP TIPS: HELPING A CHILD RESPOND TO JESUS

Helen Franklin, Steve Hutchinson and Robert Willoughby

© Scripture Union 2009
First published 2009
ISBN 978 1 84427 387 4

Scripture Union, 207–209 Queensway, Bletchley, Milton Keynes, MK2 2EB, England
Email: info@scriptureunion.org.uk
Website: www.scriptureunion.org.uk

Scripture Union, 157 Albertbridge Road, Belfast, BT5 4PS
Website: www.suni.co.uk

Scripture Union, 70 Milton Street, Glasgow, G4 0HR
Website: www.suscotland.org.uk

Scripture Union Australia
Locked Bag 2, Central Business Coast Centre, NSW 2252
Website: www.scriptureunion.org.au

Scripture Union USA
PO Box 987, Valley Forge, PA 19482
Website: www.scriptureunion.org

All rights reserved. No part of this publication may be reproduced, stored in a retrieval system, or transmitted in any form or by any means, electronic, mechanical, photocopying, recording or otherwise, without the prior permission of Scripture Union.

The right of Helen Franklin, Steve Hutchinson and Robert Willoughby to be identified as authors of this work has been asserted by them in accordance with the Copyright and Patents Act 1988.

British Library Cataloguing-in-Publication Data. A catalogue record of this book is available from the British Library.

Printed and bound in Singapore by Tien Wah Press Ltd

Logo, cover design, internal design: www.splash-design.co.uk
Internal illustrations: Colin Smithson
Typesetting: Richard Jefferson, Author and Publisher Services
Advisers: Colin Draper, John Marshall

Scripture Union is an international Christian charity working with churches in more than 130 countries, providing resources to bring the good news of Jesus Christ to children, young people and families and to encourage them to develop spiritually through the Bible and prayer.

As well as our network of volunteers, staff and associates who run holidays, church-based events and school Christian groups, we produce a wide range of publications and support those who use our resources through training programmes.

CONTENTS

Introduction		4
Part One	How people responded to Jesus in the Bible	6
Part Two	Your response to children wanting to meet Jesus	11
Part Three	Putting this into practice	20
Ten Top Tips		31
Resources		32

INTRODUCTION

Ask a Christian children's worker what is the most important thing they would want to help a child to do and they would probably say something like, 'respond to Jesus' or 'get to know Jesus'. Of course, such a worker would want to share the love of God with a child or equip them to become responsible adults and so on. But the overarching desire would be that each child we are in contact with should have a personal encounter with Jesus which transforms their life in a way that lasts for ever. So, how can we do it?

This book briefly examines what it means for a child to respond naturally to Jesus in a way that is uniquely appropriate to them. It also looks at the responsibilities that rest upon a children's worker in the privileged position of enabling a child to respond. Throughout the book, the term 'responding to Jesus' is used, but these would not be the words most children's workers would say. 'Becoming Jesus' friend', 'following Jesus' or 'becoming a Christian' would be more widely used.

The three writers of this book are evidence that we can come to Jesus in different ways, at different ages and from different backgrounds.

All through her childhood and teenage years, Helen Franklin was very familiar with God, but he was only there for the tough times such as exams. Her parents led Sunday school groups and so she was a regular in church. In her early days at college she made friends with a girl who was having something of a spiritual crisis. Helen decided that she should have one too! It seemed a good way to build a friendship. It worked, but more importantly, through this 'crisis' and the friendship, she came to know the fullness of God in Jesus. She's like Simon Peter (see page 7).

Robert Willoughby went to a Roman Catholic infant school where he was fascinated by the stories of Jesus and came to love him. Later he became a choir boy in an Anglican church, and his father sometimes came to church with him. But his experience of Jesus as a 7-year-old never developed. It was only at university, after a torrid few years, that this love for Jesus became a lifelong commitment, as he developed an understanding of Jesus that was appropriate for a 22-year-old. What finally clinched it was the way that Jesus spoke to the demon-possessed pig-minder in Mark 5. He's like Thomas (see page 8).

Steve Hutchinson's parents took him to church each Sunday and taught him to read his Bible and pray every day. He can't recall a time when he didn't know about Jesus, but remembers one special meeting of the boys' Crusader group aged 10, when the man at the front spoke about Jesus being a friend to anyone who wished to ask him. Steve says, 'At the time I didn't have many really good friends, so I loved the idea of Jesus being a true friend who would always stick by me.' Later that night in bed, he asked Jesus to be his friend. He recalls that he asked for forgiveness aged 13, committed himself to Jesus as Lord at 16 and has responded in other ways many times since. He's like Timothy (see page 9).

1 HOW PEOPLE RESPONDED TO JESUS IN THE BIBLE

In the Old Testament, God met with people in a variety of ways and their response was varied. For example, there is the story of Abraham's growth in faith up to the point of his greatest test (Genesis 22), Moses' 40 years in the desert getting straight with God (Exodus 3,4) or David's ups and downs in discipleship.

The New Testament similarly, does not encourage us to think that everyone comes to faith in Christ in exactly the same way. It's easy to think that if we follow a particular pattern or template, that will be enough. In Part One we will look at four examples of how someone began to follow Jesus and how they continued with Christ.

The apostle Paul – faith with a dramatic turnabout

Probably the most famous 'conversion' is that of the apostle Paul. Acts records it for us three times, in chapters 9, 22 and 26 – evidence of how important this event was to the early church. Paul himself offers an account as he claims his right to speak about the gospel (Galatians 1:11–24) and defends it as the truth. However, some have questioned whether we should describe his experience as a conversion, since the accounts of Paul on the road to Damascus focus just as much on his calling and commissioning as an apostle to the Gentiles: 'foreigners, kings and the people of Israel' (Acts 9:15). Paul himself might have queried whether what happened was really *conversion* at all since he didn't see it as changing his faith in order to follow a different one, but as a truer understanding and fulfilment of his Jewish faith. His experience however, did bring about a complete reorientation of his priorities and deeply affected the way he worshipped God, with Christ becoming the centre of his faith. Paul's conversion was dramatic and changed his life for ever.

This does raise the question of whether this is the most helpful model for conversion for children. For Paul it certainly was a crisis, a devastating, though ultimately joyful, experience. He was a grown man with a long history of faithful Jewish ancestors and was personally very zealous. In a very real way, Paul is unique. For children's workers to expect children to go through a similar dramatic turnaround may not only lead to the adult's own disappointment, it must also place unbearable pressure upon the children. Some adults would say that as a child they pretended that they had a dramatic response, so that their experience fitted the model and adults around them were kept happy!

This is not to deny that children do have dramatic conversions. Nor is it to deny that they might face real crises as they turn to Christ. But it must not be our only or main model for children to respond to Jesus.

Simon Peter – faith that is two steps forward, one back

When it comes to thinking about how children respond to Jesus, Simon Peter is perhaps a better place to start. All of the Gospels record Jesus calling him early on in his ministry, with the fullest account in Luke 5:1–11. Jesus asks Simon to help him and Simon Peter is astonished to find himself involved in a full-scale miracle. It seems unlikely that this was the first time he had been aware of or even met Jesus. John 1:35–42 tells us how his brother Andrew was responsible for introducing him to Jesus. Simon Peter may have addressed Jesus as 'Lord' (Luke 5:8) and Andrew may have confidently asserted that they had found the Messiah (John 1:41), but it is difficult to know what this meant to them. Jews had lots of different ideas about what or who the Messiah might be!

Not much later, Peter blurts out his famous confession, but Mark 8:27–37 reveals that, when Jesus began to talk about his suffering, Peter disagreed with him and received a very sharp rebuke for his pains.

Peter's growing comprehension reaches its lowest point as he denies his Lord three times (Mark 14:27–72) and, as far as we know, he is nowhere to be seen at the crucifixion. Thankfully John 21 records his restoration by Jesus and the early chapters of Acts reveal a changed character, full of the Holy Spirit, faith and courage.

Peter seems to be someone for whom faith is a series of passionate commitments and crises but who is short on stability. Nevertheless his faith does grow through successive rebukes and encouragements. In this way Peter resembles much more closely the experience of many children with a number of ups and downs as they grow in relationship with Christ and their understanding of faith.

Thomas – faith made firm by evidence

Thomas is, of course, another of the 12 disciples, but John's Gospel shows him to have been something of a passionate seeker. He longs to follow Jesus, though it's difficult to know what motivates his thirst for martyrdom (John 11:16). Like many others, he seems deeply thoughtful and unwilling simply to accept things at face value. Why should he? God's people were always called to exercise faith, not to be naively gullible. Israel always had enough false prophets to encourage discernment and vigorous examination. So Thomas simply asks questions and Jesus takes them seriously rather than brushing them aside or implying that they are inadmissible (John 14:1–7). Jesus speaks to him clearly and points to his experience and previous knowledge. Thomas is a very modern character. He does not take things at face value and even challenges Jesus when he is uncertain. Like many of the disciples, he is clearly puzzled by Jesus.

Of course, the famous final episode with Thomas in John 20:24–29 has given him the name 'Doubting Thomas'. This is not really fair. Thomas believed the evidence when it was presented and seems to have been quick to accept the facts before his eyes. However, he demanded proof – wanting a few answers and his questions taken seriously, just as Paul did with the people he met in Thessalonica (Acts 17:1–4). Accepting things without any thought doesn't seem to have been part of the agenda.

Some people use questions and similar objections as a cloak for other problems and will always find reasons not to believe. Yet children are naturally curious and ask questions endlessly. That is how they sort things out in their minds. Children's workers should never give up on answering questions, for children deserve respect and there may just be a chance that the child before them is a 'Thomas' – wanting credible answers to real questions. What right have we to dismiss their probing? Our responsibility is to be prepared and patient in the way that Jesus himself was with this rather challenging disciple. Our challenge is to give answers that are appropriate to children, with integrity.

Timothy – faith nurtured from birth

Timothy is a person of genuine Christian faith who needs mentoring, involvement, guidance and reassurance. After all, that is what most people need. The record seems to show that Paul's time and effort was well spent.

We know a good deal about Timothy, the travelling companion of Paul, who is even referred to by Paul as 'son'. Timothy grew up in a faith-filled home with a faithful mother and grandmother (2 Timothy

1:5). His father was a Gentile, which would explain why Timothy had not been circumcised as a baby (Acts 16:3) even though his mother's Jewish heritage would have qualified him for this. Maybe his mixed background goes some way to explain why Timothy seems to need a good deal of encouragement and help in discerning the difference between true faith and error. Paul's two letters to him (1 and 2 Timothy) are full of practical advice and help in recognising what to do about false teachers and bad practice in the church.

As a character Timothy seems rather timid and fearful (2 Timothy 1:7). This does not throw doubt upon the genuineness of his faith commitment but it helps to explain why he is 'followed up' and mentored so insistently by Paul. He becomes his co-worker (1 Thessalonians 3:2), helps him write some of his letters and is sent on a number of important assignments. Paul, in other words, seems to have thought strategically about how Timothy might grow both as a person, a Christian and a minister of the Gospel.

> **Think about…**
> As you read this book, reflect on which of these four biblical models is closest to your own response to Jesus and also closest to that of the children whose faith you seek to nurture.

So, here we have four biblical examples of people who started out in faith, grew in faith and became the people God wanted them to be in his service. The picture of faith as a way or a journey is clearly demonstrated in what we find in the biblical record.

Children are setting out on a journey of life and faith. Our task and privilege is to help them along that way.

10 *Top Tips on Helping a child respond to Jesus*

YOUR RESPONSE TO CHILDREN WANTING TO MEET JESUS

A child's response to Jesus may be stimulated by all sorts of means and at the most unexpected of times. For example:

- You have just told the story of Jesus' death on the cross at your holiday club and Sophie, aged 6, turns to you with a look of astonishment and sadness on her face. 'Jesus died!' is all that she says, but her expression tells you that she needs to talk about this a bit more. How does the conversation develop from here?
- At the end of a week of special clubs for children, Nathan, a 10-year-old tells you that he has enjoyed the activities and now believes that Jesus is God's Son. How do you reply?
- In your regular Sunday morning activity you are discovering the story of Peter preaching to the crowd on the day of Pentecost. It seems appropriate to encourage them to respond to Jesus themselves, but what do you say?

You haven't got time to think about the words to use in each of these scenarios, although thoughtful preparation may have made you aware of potential opportunities. What you say will vary according to the child who asks the question and their faith background. As in the lives of Paul, Peter, Thomas and Timothy, there will be numerous factors that lead individual children to think as they do. As children's leaders we should keep these in mind as we encourage responses to Jesus.

The child's Christian background

Sophie (see above), whose emotions were stirred by the story of Jesus' death, is the child of Christian parents. As a baby she was baptised in the local parish church, which her family attend regularly. Her parents have read Bible stories to her since she was a toddler, so this is not the first time she has heard of Jesus' death on the cross. But this is the moment at which her understanding is awakened.

Sophie is too young to grasp any idea of the link between the water sprinkled on her as a baby and the cleansing power of Jesus' death, but when her parents pray with her that night as they put her to bed, they are thrilled to hear that she wants to be Jesus' friend for ever. They thank God that this is the next stage on from the promises they made on Sophie's behalf six years earlier. These promises have become hers, by choice.

At 10 years of age, Nathan (see previous page) is old enough to make the links between baptism and belief, but as his grandmother is Jewish he knows nothing of it, having been circumcised when he was 8 days old. His parents do not have any faith but were happy for him to come to the club. The following week they drop him off at your midweek club; he says they are 'cool' about him wanting to follow Jesus, and asks you if it is true that Jesus was a Jew? Silently, you thank God that later in the term the material you use includes three outlines on Abraham!

All the members of your Sunday group have undergone a range of initiation rites, from baptism or christening through to thanksgiving or dedication to nothing at all, depending on their parents' thinking and beliefs. With a young child it may be too hard to see any connection between a faith initiation ceremony that they underwent when a baby to the response they might now want to make to Jesus. But at the appropriate age, it can be a helpful way to explain how faith grows.

Infant baptism is described as a 'sacrament of God's grace': it is as much a sign of what God offers to the child as of the hope of the parents that this baby will grow up to walk with Jesus. In some church traditions 'Christening' is considered to be the moment when the child becomes a Christian; for others, that can only come through reasoned thought and decision. For those who have been 'dedicated', making a positive response to Jesus will be another step along the pathway to faith that their parents have desired and prayed for them. Complex as it may be, we should bear these things in mind, and use them appropriately, when helping children respond to Jesus.

If a child in a church community that practises 'believer's baptism' makes a clear and positive response to Jesus, they may ask to be baptised. Is this appropriate? At what age is a child old enough to make that decision?

> **Think about…**
> Catherine is 8 and has just chosen to follow Jesus. She asks to be baptised but the church leadership are unsure and ask your advice. What will you say? You will need to consider her age, her understanding and the impact it may have on other children. What might be the implications of saying 'yes' to Catherine? And what might be the implications of saying 'no'?

The child's experience of celebrations in church
Children in the Roman Catholic Church may take communion as early as 7 or 8, with huge emphasis being placed on the first time they do this. The governing laws in the Church of England now make baptism, rather than confirmation, the door to communion, although the decision about whether or not children can take communion rests first on the bishop's stance for the diocese, and then with the choice of each individual parish. Non-conformist churches vary in their approach to the question of whether or not children are allowed to participate in communion. This can be linked with church membership. Some parents have strong and varied opinions about this too.

Being allowed to eat bread and drink wine will be no big deal for

some children, but for others it will be an important occasion, not least one that helps them to feel included as part of the church family. They will need to be well prepared for this, to have some sense of what it means, and this can be a great opportunity to talk about the ways in which it is a response to Jesus.

> **In reality…**
> When asked what they like or dislike about taking communion Michael's answer is, 'I like it because it feels as if God is here,' whilst Rachel says, 'I like getting the little snack, as I'm hungry at the end of the service!'

The child's journey through life up to now

Children go through a variety of 'rites of passage' throughout childhood: first words, first steps, first day at nursery, the move to 'big school' and then to junior school, before the enormous leap into secondary education. Year by year birthday celebrations mark the passage of time as children grasp the sense that life changes the older they become. It helps to remind them of this as you talk with them about responding to Jesus: their response needs to develop with them, not to stay as it was when first made. Of course, spiritual growth may not necessarily match physical growth. But, just as children are used to taking developmental steps forward, it is perfectly natural to help them think about responding to Jesus further or in a different way.

Faith development
Over the years various theories of faith development have been suggested. You can read much more about this in *Top Tips on Encouraging faith to grow* (SU). It is helpful to remember that faith needs to grow and develop, and that leaders or parents ought to be helping children to grow in their faith and response.

Look back at Part One to remind yourself of how Peter's faith developed from what could be seen as the cynical fisherman in Luke 5, 'We've been fishing all night and caught nothing, but if you say so…' to the fervent preacher of Acts 2, who called people to turn back to God, be baptised and receive the Holy Spirit. At the beginning Peter was somewhat reluctant to obey Jesus' command about fishing, but by Acts 5, when the Jewish Council told him to stop preaching, his bold response was, 'We don't obey men; we obey God.'

An 8-year-old child comes to you after a special event and says, 'I want to be Jesus' friend.' That's great! But two years later, during a midweek club session on Daniel's life, you would hope that the child's response to Jesus might be more along the lines of 'Jesus, I'm trying to follow you whatever happens, just like Daniel.' Each child is on their own unique faith journey.

Family influence and other background issues
The story of Timothy reminds us of the part that family can play in a child's response to Jesus. In his second letter to Timothy, Paul writes of the positive influence of both the young man's mother and grandmother, and the fact that he has known the Scriptures since infancy.

However, for some children this is not their experience. Far from being influenced for good by their parents' Christian faith, some children will have experienced the opposite and will reject Jesus or, at best, only pay lip service, being 'over-churched'. Of course there may be many children in your group with no church background or no family member who is a Christian – such as the example of Nathan on page 11 – for whom a positive response to Jesus is a natural step. Among a group of children from mixed spiritual backgrounds it may well be those with no experience of church who have the greatest expectation that God will answer their prayers and who are the keenest to move on in their faith.

However we must remember that children are the responsibility of their parents, and we must honour them in that role, not teaching children things of which their parents disapprove. We can teach them truths but not demand that they respond in a particular way, if to do so would create difficulties for them within their family. We need to have integrity in this, and also to trust God, that even if parents will not allow a child to come to a Christian group, God will still be at work in that child – not everything depends on us!

Individual or group? The influence of peer responses

What you say will also be influenced by whether you are talking with an individual or a group of children or young people. They hate being left out and some will respond in a particular way because that is how their friends have reacted. If you are talking with a group, allow each child space to make up their own mind. It will be especially important to give children an opt-out opportunity: perhaps explaining more of what is involved in the response they might make and then arranging another time to talk more when they have had time to think about it. But make it clear that they are always welcome to come back to you another time

if they ever want to change their mind! God's timing in this is going to be perfect.

> **In reality…**
> John and Sian both said they wanted to follow Jesus, so their group leader talked with them about what it meant. She then sent them home and arranged to meet them ten minutes before the next group time began, when the three of them could chat quietly (with other leaders in the room). John came as arranged, but Sian decided she wasn't ready to be a follower of Jesus, and just came to the group as usual.

Previous responses
At week-long events where there have been plenty of opportunities to respond to Jesus several times, some children may want to make the same response more than once. We might need to point out that there is no need to do so again and again. At gatherings where there has been mention of a book being given to those who respond, children are often keen just to 'get the book', or maybe, just to please you. With 'repeat responders' a Bible verse

> **Think about…**
> The speaker at a large gathering invited people of all ages to respond to Jesus, adding that children who came to the front would be given a book. One person who was trained to talk with children found himself confronted by a very young toddler in a push-chair. 'She just wanted the book,' said her mother. What would you say and do in that situation?

Top Tips on Helping a child respond to Jesus

could give assurance that if we have asked Jesus to be with us, he is already there.

There are also many children (adults as well!) who, over the years, make a series of responses to God. As leaders or parents we need to treat each step as important. We may not be aware that a child has been in this place before, and indeed they may not be aware either, but the key thing is to celebrate what they *now* believe and the response they are *now* making, and never to belittle what they have thought before. These series of responses grow into Christian commitment.

> **Think about…**
> Gavin 'became a Christian' at the ages of 5, 8 and 12. Did he get it wrong on the first two occasions? Was he not really serious? Was the leader who talked with him the third time wrong to celebrate this great event?

Your relationship with the child

If we ask children if they want to respond to Jesus in a particular way, they may do so because they know it is what *they* want. But they may equally make a particular response because they think it is what is expected of them or to please the leader. It may not be easy to discern what lies behind a child's response to God. We do well to listen to God's Holy Spirit prompting and leading us as we talk with them.

Children may respond more to a guest speaker than to regular leaders; firstly, as they hear Bible truths from a new source – it is not just their group leaders who believe in Jesus! Secondly, the visitor will have no preconceived ideas about the children's beliefs and relationships with God: they start together with a clean slate. Despite our best efforts children may be hesitant to speak of deep things with people they see week by week. Of course they don't have the words to begin a conversation but a visitor may offer openings such as, 'Come and talk to me during the next game if you want to know more about this.' The experience of Scripture Union field staff has been that both children and adults often talk more openly with them, not because they are better than their regular leaders but simply because they are not their regular leaders!

As leaders we may be harsh with ourselves or disappointed if children respond to Jesus through the work and words of someone else. But we should keep in mind Paul's comments on the subject: 'I planted the seeds, Apollos watered them, but God made them sprout and grow' (1 Corinthians 3:6,7). It does not matter who it is who plants or waters. It is God who makes the plants grow. We all have a contribution to make, but ultimately this is God's work, and we should never lose sight of that.

Evidence of the Spirit already at work
As well as listening to the Holy Spirit's prompting as we talk with children, we should also look for evidence of his work in them, and help each child to respond accordingly. How is the likeness of Jesus growing in the child? What does God seem to be doing in them now? What is the appropriate response for them to make? There is no set path for this. If Peter was astonished that the Holy Spirit fell on Cornelius and the other believers even before they had been baptised, we may be just as astonished by the Spirit's work today! Children need to make appropriate responses – appropriate to their age, background and understanding, and to what God, by his Spirit, has already done in them.

3 PUTTING THIS INTO PRACTICE

Practical steps

The following steps may appear to be rather mechanical. It is a bit like learning first aid techniques and being clear what has to be done – as soon as a medical need arises, those who have been well-trained and are confident will step forward to meet the need. They know what to do. In the same way, with these guidelines, both you and those you seek to equip will be able to confidently step forward as soon as a child expresses a desire to respond in some way to Jesus. It also keeps alive in your mind the expectation that a child may respond.

When?

It sounds obvious, but a child might respond to Jesus at any time and often on the most unexpected occasions! We might hope or pray for a response at certain times, perhaps at a holiday club or a special service, a large convention or a residential. Or we might be running a *So, Why God?* course (see page 32) to help children find answers to their questions about God, Jesus and the Bible, which could naturally lead to them wanting to respond to Jesus. But children are not restricted to any

> **Think about…**
> When we invite parents to send their children to our holiday club or residential, do we make it clear to them that one of our aims is to share the Christian faith with their children and invite them to respond to Jesus? Should we explain this and, if so, how best can we do this?

of these times. Children's workers need to be ready to help a child respond to Jesus whenever they ask.

Where?

There is no need to go somewhere private to talk with a child. In fact we should stay in view of other people, though it may be helpful to find somewhere quieter, so you can listen and talk more easily. It is most natural just to say to the child, 'Let's go and sit over there.'
Try to be at the same level as the child so as not to talk down to them.

> **In reality…**
> I shall never forget the evening I was walking with my small group of boys along the cliffs after a barbecue at Bude Beach Mission. One boy asked how to become a Christian, and before I could answer, another boy explained how he had become one a little while before.

Who?

Traditionally, it is the accepted practice that in helping a child respond to Jesus men should talk to boys and women to girls. This is a good idea, but if a child comes to you, they have probably chosen to ask you in particular on the basis of their relationship with you. It might be unhelpful if you then tell them you shouldn't talk to them but need to pass them onto someone of their own gender. It would be better to help them yourself, as they have come to you.

How?

Talking to a child about responding to Jesus should really be like talking to them about any subject that matters to them or you:
- Just be natural.
- Find out what they want to ask and do.
- Offer to help and answer their questions.
- Try to work out what they understand.

Top Tips on Helping a child respond to Jesus

- Keep it short and simple.
- Let the children set the pace of the conversation.
- There is no need to share lots of Bible verses, or go through a checklist of Bible doctrine.
- Don't pressurise them to respond, but offer them help if they are ready but don't know quite what to do.
- Don't feel it all depends on you. It is the Holy Spirit's job. He uses different people to help us respond to God at different times.
- If you need to explain how to respond to Jesus because a child has come to you at a holiday club or residential, use the same explanation that has been used during the activity. (This should be talked about and agreed in the team preparation.)
- A prayer card may be available, in which case you can explain what that means and ask the child if they understand it, and if that is what they want to say to Jesus. But don't worry if it isn't what they want to say, just ask what they *would* like to tell Jesus.
- Encourage children to pray out loud themselves. If you are going to pray, ask the children if this is OK.
- As a general rule, if our activities are going to invite children to respond, always make it as easy to opt out as to join in the response.

In reality…
Becky, aged 11, said that the way she would want to help children be friends with Jesus was to help them know what to say to him. Sometimes children know what they want to do, but don't know how to say it in a prayer or how to talk with God.

It may be helpful to have a booklet available, (for example, see the inside back cover), for children who want to know more about responding to Jesus, to help them make up their minds and to help them be clear what it is all about. Suggest the child takes the booklet and reads it with a parent, family member or friend, so that they are aware of what their child is thinking about. Offer to pray with them the next time you see them, if they want your help, or say that they can do it on their own if they prefer. Encourage them to come back to you when they are ready.

You will also want to make sure that the child understands that God's Spirit comes to be with anyone who is a follower of Jesus. He helps us live in a way that pleases God, making us aware of what is right and wrong. He helps us talk with God and also talk about Jesus with others. He is indeed 'God with

Think about…
Imagine a child comes to you and asks how they can become a Christian. What would you say?

In reality…
One evening at the Lagger camp, two girls asked for a prayer card after the tent group times. I asked if they had ever prayed a prayer like this before. They both said they hadn't. One said she was a Christian, but wanted to pray this prayer, the other wanted to use this prayer to become a Christian. I was happy to help them both to respond to Jesus in the way they wanted.

Top Tips on Helping a child respond to Jesus

us'. Using the prayer on the card on page 25 will prompt you to explain who the Holy Spirit is.

Following Jesus comes at a cost and although you do not want to major on this, any new follower needs to know that now they belong to Jesus their behaviour will change – just as Zacchaeus changed his lifestyle after tumbling down the tree to meet Jesus. It could be seen as though they have joined Jesus' team, are identified by his colours and play by his rules. This will make them different from others and from how they were. The work of the Holy Spirit is evidence of this.

It is good practice to explain how to respond to Jesus when children are all together. This would include what to say to God in a prayer. For some children, this may be enough as they know what to do and say. For others you might need to offer help and/or give them a prayer card. If you give a child a card, also ask if they have any questions. Suggest they take the card to read somewhere quiet on their own, then talk about it to their parents/carers or a sympathetic adult before they pray.

Think about…

Do you include an opportunity for children to respond in your holiday club, residential or special event? How could you do this so that all children have a chance to respond if they wish, without putting undue pressure on them?

What can I say to Jesus to become his friend?

Jesus, I want to be your friend.
Thank you that you love me.
Thank you for living in the world and dying on the cross for me.
I'm sorry for the wrong things I have done.
Please forgive me and let me be your friend.
Please let the Holy Spirit help me be more like you.
Amen

This card belongs to

. . . .

Date . . . .

This card will remind you what you said to Jesus.

If you prayed this prayer and are really serious about being friends with Jesus, we would like to know, so that we can help you. Ask your parent or carer to fill in the details below, tear along the dotted line and give it back to the person who gave the card to you.

Your name . . . .

Your address . . . .

. . . .

. . . .

Postcode . . . .

Your age . . . .

> **In reality…**
> A 9-year-old girl asked an inexperienced children's worker how to become a Christian. He went right through a booklet and then gave her the choice to pray or to go away to think about it. She couldn't get away fast enough! She might simply have been asking, 'If someone wanted to become a Christian sometime, how would they do it?' rather than wanting to respond herself. The children's worker never gave her the chance to tell him.

Creating the right environment

Listen, listen, listen

It is vitally important to listen to the child. One Scripture Union evangelist says, 'I can guess why you have come to talk to me, but you tell me.' Think of open, gentle and honest questions that encourage the child to tell you what they want to do, or to say to Jesus. Listen to what they say, then try to help in an appropriate way. At the same time, listen to God, who puts thoughts into our mind to help us say the right thing.

> **In reality…**
> When asked why she wanted to come to Jesus, a girl said that her Nan had just died and the vicar at the funeral had said that Nan was now 'with Jesus'. She wanted to be with her Nan, so needed to come to Jesus. The girl, at that point, needed bereavement counselling, not a prayer for salvation.

> **In reality…**
> A 5-year-old girl heard the story of Nicodemus being told he needed to be born again. 'Do I need to get back in my Mum's tummy?' she asked. Another boy, hearing the phrase 'asking Jesus into your heart', asked, 'If I have a heart transplant, will I have to ask Jesus in again?'

Language and imagery

Think about the language you use in explaining what could be seen as abstract concepts. In general, children think literally and concretely until they are 10 or 11 years old. For example, to most children, the heart is the pump that pushes the blood round our bodies, not the seat of our will or emotions, so 'asking Jesus into your heart' can be hard to understand.

For a clear understanding of this, read *Top Tips on Explaining the cross to children* (SU), see the inside front cover.

Pastoral issues

A child who responds to Jesus does so in the context of their home background and their past – see page 15. For example, if their parents are not Christians, how will they react to the child's response? We would not want to put the child in any sort of danger or create family conflict. It has been suggested that the child should talk to their parents before they pray in response to Jesus, but the child may want you to explain it instead. This is an opportunity for you to make clear you are not pressurising the child, but are offering to help them, if this is what they want to do. Many parents will be glad about this but others may be opposed to any positive response to God. You must respect the parent's position.

Top Tips on Helping a child respond to Jesus

In the context of a child telling you what they feel or want to do, they may tell you about something bad that is happening to them, which they may ask you to keep secret. Explain that there are some secrets, such as when someone is getting hurt, that you can't keep. If the child persists in telling you, you must tell the Safeguarding Children Coordinator for the activity. They should know how to pass this on to the local safeguarding authorities who will decide what needs to be done, if anything. You can always get advice on this from the Churches' Child Protection Advisory Service on 0845 120 45 50 (24-hour helpline).

Other faiths
If a child's family is from another faith background, their parents may be happy for their child to be with godly people and to learn more about God and the Bible, but would not want their child to become a Christian. Keep parents involved and be open with them about what you are

> **In reality...**
> Natasha, from a Muslim family, came to a residential. Her mother told a team member that she was happy for Natasha to come on the holiday, but she didn't want us to make her a Christian because she wanted her to grow up a good Muslim.

discussing with their child. Honour the parent's decision even if it is that the child shouldn't make any response to Jesus. Don't be

28 *Top Tips on Helping a child respond to Jesus*

surprised if the child stops coming after you have spoken about this. Other children from the same faith background may stop coming at the same time. Whatever happens, continue to show love for the child and their family and pray for them. For more information, read *Top Tips on Welcoming children of other faiths* (SU) - see inside front cover, or visit www.scriptureunion.org.uk/youthencounter to find out about Youth Encounter.

Special needs
All children are special to God and all are capable of responding to Jesus in different ways, whatever their learning abilities. Working with children with special needs is a privilege which can bring different experiences. If necessary, seek specialist advice and support. For more information, see *Top Tips on Welcoming special children* (SU) – see the inside front cover.

> **In reality…** One church specifically designed a discipleship course for a young man with severe disabilities. They used the same communication methods he knew from school. He didn't speak, but was able to choose between options presented in pictures. He loved the Bible stories and songs used to explain the Christian faith to him. The leaders and his parents were convinced that he had made a real response to Jesus. This led to his baptism.

Follow up
Making a response to Jesus is just the beginning – or just one step on the way. Any child who has responded to Jesus needs help and nurture to get to know Jesus.

As a child has probably been encouraged to respond to Jesus by praying to him, it is natural to encourage them to continue talking with him about everything in their lives. Reassure them that Jesus loves to listen to them however they are feeling. He will forgive them if they think they have let him down and will help them when things are tough.

It is important that they become part of a church in the best way possible for them. This may mean making arrangements with a church group to help them feel able to join in. It may be that the after-school club is their church or the Christian community created by a residential holiday becomes their church community.

Any child or young person responding to Jesus needs to discover the Bible for themselves, so they can learn more about Jesus. The Bible is a large and challenging book even for adults, so most children need help and practical support. Introduce them to a child-friendly version of the Bible. Scripture Union publishes many resources to guide Bible reading - see the inside back cover.

At this time in a child's life, you have been able to guide them in their response to Jesus. Others may have already walked with them and, in the future, there will be those who help to nurture this, or further responses. Continue to pray for them and maintain contact where possible. Above all, go on trusting that Jesus himself, who has reached out to them in response, will continue to do so.

TOP TIPS

- Listen carefully to the child

- Find out how they want to respond to Jesus

- Offer simple, practical help, maybe some words to pray

- Don't pressurise them into a response

- Use appropriate language and be natural

- Be aware that the child is on a journey and may have already responded in some way to Jesus

- Involve the child's parents

- Talk to the child in a safe place, in view of others

- Be especially sensitive if the child's family is from another faith

- Whatever happens, continue to pray for and support the child

RESOURCES

Resources to use with children

Steve Hutchinson, *So why God?*, SU, 2007, a 12-session midweek club programme that explores what it means to follow Jesus, for 5–11s
Robert Willoughby, *So, who is God?*, SU, 2006, answers to 30 real questions that children have asked about God
See inside back cover for details of SU booklets to use with children

Guidance for leaders

*Pretty much everything you need to know about...*series
Draper, Franklin and O'Shea, *Working with 5–7s*, SU, 2007
Saunders and Porritt, *Working with 8–10s*, SU, 2004
Williams and Stephenson, *Working with 11–14s*, SU, 2004

Francis Bridger, *Children finding faith*, SU/CPAS, 2000
Peter Brierley, *Reaching and keeping tweenagers*, Christian Research, 2002
Ron Buckland, *Children and the Gospel*, SUA, 2001
Paul Butler, *Reaching children*, SU, 1992
Ed John Collier, *Child Theology at work in the church*, The Child Theology Movement, 2009
Penny Frank, *Every child, a chance to choose*, Children's Ministry, 2002
David Staal, *Leading kids to Jesus*, Zondervan, 2006